White Gloves
and
Party Manners

White Gloves
and
Party Manners

by
Marjabelle Young and
Ann Buchwald

Illustrated by Christiane

ROBERT B. LUCE, INC.   BRIDGEPORT, CT.

To our children
Joel, Jacqueline, Connie and Jennifer

INTRODUCTION

This may be the first book you ever read about manners. It will tell you how to act when you are with other people — your own friends your age, or grown-ups — how to act at parties, at home, school, when you go out to dinner or to the theater, and to all the other interesting places you will be going as you grow older.

It will tell you what to do and what to say to make people like you more and to make yourself more at ease at times when you might be nervous and unsure about what you are saying or doing.

Good manners are simply polite, kind ways to behave with others. Manners are easy to learn, and they never change. They will be just the same when you are a teenager, or when you get to be a grown-up.

We wrote this book for little girls (and their brothers) because we know from raising our own children just how important manners can be — not just when you are all dressed up and wearing white gloves, but *all* the time.

You don't have to read this book all at once. Just read the parts that interest you most, or read the parts that you think will be most helpful. You can always read it just before you go out to dinner, or to a party, so you'll remember just how to act when you get there.

We hope this book will help you now, and when you get older. Someday, perhaps, when you are a beautiful young lady, all dressed up in a flowing gown and long white gloves, you will be glad you read this book, because then you will be completely at ease, and have a wonderful time.

WASHINGTON, D. C. 1965   MARJABELLE YOUNG AND
ANN BUCHWALD

CONTENTS

Chapter I

GOOD MANNERS

Manners are an important part of getting along with your friends and family, teachers in school, and strangers you may meet. Being friendly and polite is probably something you do most of the time, but it's a good idea to follow these helpful hints.

YOU WILL GET ALONG WITH:

Your own friends when you admire their good points and try to overlook their faults. Be kind; not bossy, boastful or selfish. Learn to keep a secret or a promise. Return what you borrow, and share things. If you make a mistake, admit it. If you hurt someone's feelings, say you're sorry. When someone hurts your feelings, accept the apology and try to forget angry words. Don't play favorites with your friends. You never whisper to one person in front of others.

Older people who will see how friendly and respectful you are. Whenever an older man or woman comes into a room, stand up. You *always* stand up when you are being introduced to someone — your own age or older, boy or girl. Use people's names when you answer questions—not just "Yes" or "No," but "Yes, Mrs. Brown" or "No, Aunt Mary." If you don't remember an older person's last name, say "Yes,

Sir" or "Yes, ma'am." Try not to eavesdrop, but if you hear adults talking don't repeat what they say, in your own home or anywhere else. You don't criticize another's house or clothes or possessions, or make giggly comments.

Teachers, instructors or anyone who is trying to teach you because you listen quietly and are willing to learn. If you do well in school, music, sports, or scouting, be thankful for their help.

You will also get along with:

Doctors, dentists and their nurses who appreciate you because you are courteous, patient and as brave as you can be. Treat them like helpful friends, not enemies trying to hurt you. Be on time for appointments.

Those who serve you. Waiters, waitresses or bus drivers are glad to help especially if you say "Please" and "Thank You" when you order or ask for some service. Respect their work and appreciate what they do for you.

Newcomers in your school or neighborhood who are glad they met you because you make them feel wanted, not out-of-place or alone. It doesn't matter if:

They go to a different school or church.

Their speech or clothes is different.

Their parents are divorced or separated.

They have more or less money than your parents.

Their color or race is different.

They don't know as much about manners as you do!

MEETINGS, GREETINGS AND GOODBYES

To introduce means to share someone you know and like with at least one other person. *To be introduced* is the proper way to be shared with others. You have probably already made introductions without realizing it. When you brought home your first school friend and said, "Mother, this is Jenny Jones," that was an introduction. Now, as you learn a few more rules about introductions, you will grow into a more perfect hostess, a more popular guest and a more thoughtful friend. Being sure of what to say is the first secret of making introductions. The second is to speak so others can hear you. Remember to speak slowly. Then words and names will come to you without hesitation.

There are two ways to introduce people. The less formal way is to say, "This is Jane Jones," or "This is Eddie Smith." It is a fine way for young children to introduce their young friends, particularly to their own family or to others their age. The more grown-up phrase is "May I present Jane Jones." And it makes anyone you introduce feel twice as proud, twice as important to you. In your life, you will introduce thousands of people to each other, but your introductions will all fall within one of three groups.

In Group One—Introduce the Younger Person to the Older One

You will automatically do this correctly if you *look at* the person who is older — your mother, father, aunt or teacher — while you say his or her name: "Mother, this is," and then turn to the younger person and say his or her name, "Nancy Smith."

Another example: (Your teacher) "Miss Jones, may I present my brother, Joel Long."

In Group Two — Introduce the Less Important Person to the More Important

You first look at the teacher, the doctor, the Mayor or the dignitary while you say his name, "Doctor Brown, this is my friend Timmy Jones." Although they are not less important, the same rule applied when you introduce *your parents* to people such as teachers, coaches or a friend's mother. You say, "Mrs. Brown, may I present my mother." You do not say your parent's last name unless it is different from your own.

In Group Three—Introduce the Boy to the Girl

First, you look at the girl and say "Nancy, this is George Brooks." Then turn, look at the boy, and to tell him Nancy's last name you say, "Nancy Smith."

When a girl is sixteen or older, she skips from Group One to Group Three. The man is then introduced to HER even if he is older. You say, "Mary, this is my father. Dad, this is Mary Williams." The only exception to the sixteen-or-over rule is when the man is of particular importance: a Bishop, Senator, Mayor or someone with a title.

The very first thing to do when *you* are introduced is stand up! It shows friendship to those your own age and respect to older people. In fact, as soon as an adult enters the room, you should rise, even if you have to wait a few moments for introductions to begin. Only when a girl is sixteen or over may she remain seated.

Next, you *look at* the person to whom you are introduced, smile and say "How do you do" or "Hello, Jane." You don't have to say anything more unless you want to talk.

Boys always shake hands with boys or men when they are introduced. If a girl or woman offers her hand to him,

4

he shakes it, but he doesn't reach for it. Girls seldom shake hands with other girls. Usually they smile and say "Hello, Jane" or "How do you do." However, girls should be prepared to shake hands with an older woman who extends her hand.

A charming practice for a girl of twelve or older is to extend her hand when introduced to an older man. In other words, you make the *first gesture* to shake hands with a man, but wait for an older woman to lead the way.

The curtsy is the equivalent of shaking hands for girls twelve or under. In fact, part of a curtsy involves shaking hands. A curtsy is a form of respect to the adult you greet or meet. It is also something active and graceful to do during that first moment you might be feeling embarrassed or shy—or wonder how to please the person you are meeting.

Here is how you make a curtsy: Think of doing a little dance step. Place your right foot tip-toe behind your left heel, and a little to the left of it. Then bend your knees to do a quick dip. Try it—dip down, not too far; now up, straight as a princess. At the moment you start the curtsy, you extend your right hand to the older persons who shakes it as you do the dip.

How to say goodbye. The same courtesy you show when you are introduced to people should be shown when they leave. You stand up, shake hands or curtsy, and say "Goodbye, Mrs. Brown" or "Goodbye, Mary." It is always nice to add "Thank you for coming over," or "That was fun," if it is a friend your age. Then you walk to the door with her. When you stand up and say goodbye politely you make anyone feel the visit was important to you.

A few special introductions. Most adults are addressed as "Miss," "Mr.," or "Mrs." You repeat it when you say their names. But some important people have titles which you

6

will want to add after you say "How do you do." The main ones are for:

A Protestant Minister: "How do you do, Sir."

A Catholic Priest or Nun: "How do you do, Father O'Brien," or "How do you do, Father." "How do you do, Sister," or "How do you do, Sister Alberta."

A Rabbi: "How do you do, Rabbi Weiss," or just "How do you do, Rabbi."

A Congressman: "How do you do, Mr. Lindsay."

A Judge (not in the Supreme Court): "How do you do, Judge Jones."

A Judge (of the Supreme Court): "How do you do, Justice White," or "How do you do, Mr. Justice."

An Ambassador: "How do you do, Mr. Ambassador."

An Ambasador's Wife: "How do you do, Mrs. Attwood."

A Mayor: "How do you do, Mr. Mayor," or "How do you do, Mayor Berkeley."

A Governor: "How do you do, Governor Walsh."

A Senator: "How do you do, Senator Smith," or "How do you do, Senator."

The Vice President of the United States: "How do you do, Mr. Vice President."

The Wife of the Vice President of the United States: "How do you do, Mrs. Adams."

The President of the United States: "How do you do, Mr. President."

The Wife of the President of the United States: "How do you do, Mrs. Wilson."

And should you ever meet a King or a Queen, you say "How do you do, Your Majesty."

THE FINE YOUNG ART OF CONVERSATION

How many times have you wished a puppy could talk? Why? Because then he would be closer to you and a better friend. You would know more about him and have more fun being together.

Conversation at parties, at play, in your own home or out of it, is like that. When you express yourself, you share yourself with your friends and family.

Starting a conversation sometimes seems difficult, and the temptation is to wait for someone else to speak first. But it is a mark of good manners to know how to start. (We have a friend whose father offers ten cents to any child who starts a conversation during dinner with the person on his left or right. The father says, "It's easy. Just look at the fruit bowl in the center of the table and ask, 'Which do you like best, apples or pears?' ")

Questions are easiest. Turn to your friend and ask what he or she did that day, or what school is like, or where he went for summer vacation, or if he has a pet.

Some questions are to be avoided, especially if they are about money ("How much money does your father make?" "How much did that cost?"), or personal things ("Why is your sister so fat?" "Why do you have only one car?"). Any question you wouldn't want to answer yourself should never be asked.

Answer questions with more than a mere "yes" or "no." Help conversations along. Add an interesting fact if the conversation is about school, church, friends, hobbies or sports.

Listen to others. It encourages them to talk. If you listen, you can learn. Then, too, you don't have to ask "What?" so often.

Avoid unpleasant topics at the table. When you talk about accidents, illnesses or bodily functions, appetites are spoiled. You wouldn't want to eat while cleaning up a cut finger, would you? Well, no on else will want to either, if you tell about it during dinner.

Interrupting is like pushing someone off the sidewalk. It's a shock and no one likes it. Even if it takes patience, you should wait for your turn to speak.

If you whisper in front of others, you cut out everyone else in the room as surely as if you'd chased them out and closed the door. When you have something to say to only one person, wait until you are alone with him. A whisper always sounds like bad news or something unpleasant to those left out.

Loud talk is not conversation. It usually means you haven't enough to say, or you're ashamed of what you are saying or doing. Teasing is a good example of this. Have you ever heard a child make fun of someone in a quiet, polite voice? No, because it's impossible to! Loud voices are not pleasant—they make other people uncomfortable.

Say no or disagree if you want to. This *is* part of conversation. But add "No, I'm sorry," or "No, thank you," or "No, not right now," or "No, I am not allowed" or "No, I don't think so." Then you can express an idea or preference without offending your friends.

When you brag you show off in words. If you excel at something, your friends will find it out very fast and then *they'll* do the boasting for you. They'll also boast that you're their friend!

Tell the truth. For lack of interesting things to say, don't exaggerate, fib or tell a lie. When friends find out, they will hesitate to trust you even when you *are* telling the truth.

Try to think of pleasant things to say. Anyone can be a fault-finder; that's easy. No one is perfect. It takes good manners and a special friendliness to see the good points in people. Don't ridicule, make fun of others' clothes, relatives, appearance or houses. Don't say "You always . . ." because the only answer to that is an angry "I do not" and anger turns conversation into a battle.

10

Compliments are like gifts. When you receive a compliment say "Thank you." Accept a compliment as you would a gift, with appreciation and graciousness.

Try to compliment a friend privately, not in front of others, unless you want to find a compliment for everyone present.

Avoid monopolizing the conversation. Instead of a parade of "I, I, I's," say "I think," "Let's" or "It seems." Bring others into the conversation by saying, "I can ski, can you?" If you are greedy about conversation, you will find yourself without listeners.

DOORWAY MANNERS

When the doorbell rings and your parents are near it, it is best to ask permission to answer the door. If the answer is "Yes, please," don't be in a rush. Open it gently and give yourself time to find out who it is and what to do.

If it's a family friend, neighbor or someone you know, first say "Hello," then immediately invite him in, saying, "Please come in." Then show him where to sit while you call the person he wants. Don't shout from where you are standing, but find the person who is wanted. Never take the visitor along with you on the search from room to room.

If it's a stranger at the door, say "Hello" and listen to the request or ask, "What can I do for you?" ("What is it, please?") Do not invite him in the house, but say "Please wait here." Then close the door and call a grown-up.

If it is the postman, milkman, or a delivery man, he will not expect to be invited in unless it is unusually bad weather. In that case, he will merely step inside the door and wait to conduct his business.

When you ring someone's doorbell, do it firmly but not forever. Then wait, because it often takes a while to get to the door from another part of the house. You may ring a second time after a wait, but then if there is no answer, give up for the time being.

When someone answers, wait to be invited into the house— don't just push your way in. Look for and use the door mat, even in the summer. If the person you want isn't there, say "Thank you, would you tell Mary that Jane Jones stopped by?" before you walk away. Don't vanish like a ghost without giving your name or leaving a message.

UNSEEN MANNERS

Sometimes you want people to know how you feel, even when they can't see your face or know you personally. When you learn the proper way to use the telephone or write a thank-you letter, it will be easy for anyone to know how friendly you are.

Telephones. What people think about you when you talk on the telephone depends on your voice. It must not be too low, slow or lazy—but certainly not too fast or loud either. Your voice will be clear and natural if you imagine the person you're talking to is sitting beside you on a sofa.

When you make a telephone call:

Dial carefully and correctly. It's a good idea to have the number written down in front of you.

Wait for a few rings before giving up and hanging up.

When someone answers, say "Hello" before you say another word. Then say, "This is Jane Smith. May I please speak to Sue?" Even if your friend or parent answers the phone and recognizes your voice, you must always say who you are.

When the person you call isn't there, don't just hang up or mumble, "Oh." Be sure to give your name, and say you will call again, or ask to be called back, please.

Say "Goodbye" before you hang up. It is the only way someone knows you intend to stop talking. Then hang up, don't wait to hear if your friend has also hung up.

Above all, don't use the telephone to play jokes, or to annoy people.

When you answer the telephone:

When it rings, don't race or wrestle for the phone. Even if you win, you'll be out of breath!

Say "Hello" in a pleasant voice as soon as you pick up the receiver. This tells the caller someone is paying attention.

If the call is for you, there is only one answer, "This is Jane"—not "This is me," "This is she" or just "Speaking."

If the call is for someone else in the house, say "Just a moment, please," and then notify the person who is being called.

If the call is for someone not at home, say "He is not here. Would you like to leave a message?" Be sure to take the message exactly right. Don't be afraid to ask the caller to repeat the message. Say "Goodbye" before you hang up.

Try to limit the length of your telephone calls; or your family will have to do it for you! A telephone is one of those things you share with other people in the house. When you make a call, you should be the one to say goodbye first. And until you are twelve years old, don't make telephone calls after dinner. They may disturb your friends' parents who might be having guests or a party.

14

Letters. Letters are like short visits with people on paper. They should be nice to look at, natural and interesting—the way you would be if you were there in person. People answer you when you talk to them; and they will answer your letters, too, when you remember these simple rules:

Start with the date in the upper corner of the paper.

Write a salutation on a line by itself — "Dear Mother," "Dear Uncle Jim," or "Dear Sue," before you continue the letter. It is the same as saying "hello."

Write clearly and carefully. Send the very best example of your handwriting. It shows the person who receives the letter how much you've grown.

Write what you would say if the person weren't so far away. Even if it is a thank-you note, add some interesting fact or some family news.

End a letter with more than just your name. For a closing, write "With love," or "Yours truly," or "Affectionately," depending on how close a friend it is, and how you feel about that person.

Address envelopes clearly, and leave room for postage in the upper right corner. Center the name, street and city lines in the middle of the envelope; then leave a frame of white around them.

Answer your mail and you will get more letters. When someone has taken the time to write to you, return the compliment by answering within two weeks.

Thank-You Notes are some of your most important letters. They may be brief, but they should be kind, cheerful and prompt. When you receive a gift by mail, you should

say "thank you" in writing as quickly as you would say it if the gift were handed to you.

When you have stayed with someone as a house guest, write within the first week after you return, to thank the family for its hospitality. Even if you were a little homesick while visiting your friend's house, don't mention it in your thank-you letter. Before you end the note, try to add one or two lines of something that will be of interest to your friend.

FOR BOYS ONLY

Boys are lucky: They have their own rules of politeness. They are very simple, and not too hard to learn.

A boy stands up promptly whenever a girl, or a woman— or an older man—enters the room or crosses it to talk to him.

A boy opens the door for a woman and then steps back to let her enter the house, the room, or the restaurant first.

A boy seats a women at the table this way: He stands behind the chair and pulls it out far enough for her to get between it and the table. Then as the woman bends her knees, he pushes the chair gently toward the table so it will be there for her to sit on.

A boy remains standing at the table until a woman or girl is seated. In a group, boys wait for their dinner partners to be seated before they sit down. When a girl or woman approaches his table to talk, a boy stands up and remains standing as long as she is there.

A boy gets into a car after a woman or girl — and gets out first.

A boy shakes hands each time he is introduced to a man, a boy or any woman who first offers her hand. A boy develops a firm, brief, handshake all his own—not a bone-crusher nor such a weak one his hand seems injured. A boy always looks at the person whose hand he is shaking. He never looks down, or away from the other person's face.

A boy gives the order to the waiter or waitress, after first asking a girl or a woman what she would like—just like Dad does when he is there.

A boy carries packages for his mother, or any woman or girl he's walking with.

A boy removes his hat when he is introduced, when he stops to talk on the street and when he enters a house or an apartment building elevator. He keeps his hat on in public buildings and elevators—it takes up less room on his head than held in his hand. He removes his hat when entering all Christian churches.

A boy helps a woman remove her coat in church, the theater or a restaurant. Then he either hangs it up for her or takes it to the checkroom.

A boy gives up his seat to a woman standing near him on a bus, subway or train.

A boy says "please excuse me" or "I'm sorry" when he passes in front of others—not just, "oops," or worse still, "Look out!"

A boy walks on the curb side of the street when he is with a woman.

Chapter II

GOOD TABLE MANNERS

When you were a baby, you were alone in a high chair. With a spoon clasped in your little fist, you struggled to put food into your mouth. Whatever missed your mouth landed all over and around you. People laughed and gladly cleaned up after your "feeding." If you ate your vegetables, that was all that mattered. You didn't eat *with* anyone— you just ate.

Now you are growing up and rarely eat by yourself. Usually you are at a table with your family, or with school friends. Soon you will be a guest at dinner parties, luncheons, teas in other people's homes, in restaurants and hotels. You will be among adults, and at times you will be the youngest one present.

You will see that there is more to eating than the food itself. *How you eat*—and *how you behave* while eating— are as important as eating. Why? Because good table manners let people around you enjoy their meals: the good food and the lively talk around the dinner table. You look better while you are eating, neater, more graceful and more sure of yourself. Good manners take the struggle out of eating and make it easy and enjoyable, whether it's an afternoon snack or a dinner party.

BEFORE YOU START TO EAT. Think of how many kinds of food we eat, and how many hours we spend eating each year. Eating is fun, not just because you're hungry—like the goldfish swimming around his bowl eating the same food each day—but because eating makes you happy. Most table manners are simple, sensible ways to avoid doing things that spoil appetites and take away the pleasure of eating. These are the ways to avoid ugliness at the table:

Be clean and neat. Wash your hands and face, brush your hair, and make a quick change from any dirty clothes before dinner is announced. Then you will be as pleasant to look at as the food is to eat.

Be prompt. When dinner is ready, you should be, too. You know what time dinner is usually served and you ought to be sure to be home, and ready for dinner. If you are involved in a game, or an errand, finish it later. Otherwise, you are rude to the person who prepared the food—and to those waiting to eat it.

Find your place. When you are a guest at a small party, the hostess will usually tell you where to sit. Sometimes, however, there will be a place card. It is usually placed on your napkin. Remove it as soon as you are seated and place it on the table above your plate.

Be patient. As a young guest, wait for older people to be seated before sitting down. Once you are seated, sit straight—with your chair pulled in to the table and wait for others to be seated. Do not tip or tilt a chair backward while you're waiting, nor throw your arm over the back of the chair. Hungry as you may be, do not take a little bite of bread to tide you over. A well-behaved guest does not play with silver or glassware or make nervous noises. Keep your hands folded in your lap until service starts. Just try it. Automatically, your posture will be perfect and your elbows at your side where they belong.

20

BLESSING BEFORE MEALS

Before you even touch your napkin, glance at the hostess to see if a grace will be said. If so, listen with your head bowed and say "Amen," if you wish. Then pick up your napkin.

NAPKINS

The place for a napkin is in your lap, not around your neck, unless special food like spaghetti requires it. You usually find your napkin on your plate. If the first course is already on the table, your napkin will be beside the plate. You unfold it only half-way if it is a large dinner napkin; all the way if it is a smaller, luncheon one. To keep food off the rims, use your napkin to pat (not rub) your mouth before you drink from the glass or cup. Your napkin stays on your lap throughout the meal. When you are ready to leave the table, leave the napkin—slightly crumpled but never refolded—on the table at either side of your place.

WHEN YOU ARE SERVED

When you are a guest, you will often be served food from a serving dish with a special fork and spoon on the serving plate. You will always be served from your left

21

side. As the dish is offered, turn slightly, pick up the serving *spoon* in your *right hand* and the *fork* in your *left hand*. Use the spoon to take up the food and fork to steady it as you transfer it to your plate. Then replace the fork and spoon, side by side, in the serving dish or on the platter so that handles stay clear of food. Always take what is nearest you and never search around for your favorite piece. If it is necessary to cut, do it with the spoon. If the food had been divided in the kitchen, don't try to improve on the job.

When you are served something you *don't* like, take a small amount and keep your secret. No comment is necessary. Do not thank a maid who serves you; but you do say "No, thank you," when you wish to refuse a second helping. You never have to apologize or explain why. As each course is finished, the maid will remove your plate— again from the left side. Usually only water and other liquids are served and removed from the right side.

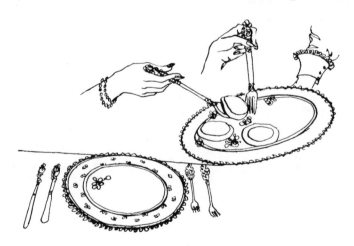

WHEN TO BEGIN

Unless your hostess has told you to go ahead, wait until she has been served and begins eating before you begin.

When there are more than six, the hostess will tell you to begin after several people have been served so that food will not get cold. When there are guests in your home, wait until they have been served before you begin eating. Even when there are no guests at the table, it is nice to wait for your parents to begin before you start.

BEING A GOOD DINNER PARTNER

The day you left the lonely high chair you were made a member of the table-group. It was a big compliment! But now, you have to cooperate with others during meals, even at home. You must learn to share attention as well as food. If you just sit there, staring or daydreaming, you put a wall between yourself and those next to you. So when you first sit down, say something friendly or interesting to the person on your left or right—not to someone you might know better down at the end of the table. The people *next* to you are your partners during dinner, and your attention goes to them. That means listening, too—because you usually learn something interesting when you listen.

Take small enough bites so that you can answer questions without a long delay before you can talk. Learn to answer briefly with just a little food in your mouth; *never,* never chew with your mouth open.

Be relaxed, but keep your elbows off the table whenever you are eating or have eating implements in either hand. Even if your meat is hard to cut, your elbows stay at table level—they must not pop up like birds' wings. It's wonderful to enjoy food, but you don't have to smack your lips to prove it. And you don't have to guard your plate by circling it with your arm. Do not reach across anyone's place for any reason. Instead say, "May I please have the salt?"

and it will be passed to you. If you drop a knife or fork, leave it until the meal is over—and ask for another if you need it. In a restaurant, don't pick it up at all.

Even in candlelight or the dim lights of a restaurant, remember that your dinner partners see your plate as well as their own. Don't shock them with a mashed-up, mixed-up, mud-pie plate.

AVOID EMBARRASSMENT

Know how to take things out of your mouth. Don't try to hide an olive or a fruit pit or a fish bone behind a napkin. Just chew off most of the fruit, olive, or fish and remove the pit or bone with your fingers. But slide a piece of meat you can't chew onto your fork and then place it on the side of your plate.

If you choke a little, take a sip of water. If you burp, don't make a big joke of it. If you have to blow your nose, do so quietly and as briefly as possible. If you have to leave the table for an emergency, just say "Please, may I be excused," and leave without going into details.

When you want to rest a bit, butter some bread, or take a drink, place your knife and fork in a way that shows you intend to continue eating. This is called *Rest Position* and the fork prongs are always down curved over the knife. You may even give your elbows a rest on the table at this point if you do it gracefully.

When you are finished, don't push your plate away from you or say "I'm through" or "I'm stuffed." Just place your knife and fork in the *Finished Position*, side by side with fork prongs *Down*.

BASIC COURSES

Bananas are perhaps the only food everyone can eat without practice. Even baby monkeys seem to have perfect banana-manners. But many foods served at a table are eaten in definite ways and with definite implements. This is not to make eating difficult; but to make it easier, more orderly and nicer to watch. Even the silver has its order: You start eating with the spoon, fork or knife farthest away from your plate, and work in toward the plate as the meal goes on. Here are the basic courses and most accepted ways to eat them.

A COCKTAIL COURSE OF SEAFOOD

Is eaten this way:

Use the small seafood or oyster fork only. Usually you find this special fork farthest to the right of your plate, to separate it from regular size forks. If you have to cut a piece of

25

seafood, do it with the fork only. When you are finished, place the fork on the little plate, not in the seafood cup.

A COCKTAIL COURSE OF FRUIT

Is eaten this way:

Use the small spoon farthest to the right of your plate. When you are finished, place the spoon on the plate, not in the fruit cup.

A SOUP COURSE

Looks like this: *Is eaten this way:*

Use the soup spoon, which is always a large one found on the right of the knives. The soup spoon is held in the right hand with the thumb across the top. It is not held like a pencil because it might flip over and spill the soup. The spoon should be dipped away from you, and the soup sipped silently from the side or end of the spoon. Dipping away prevents splashing your clothes. To get the last mouthful, you may tip the soup plate away from you. When you are finished, leave the spoon on the plate, not in the soup dish.

26

A BUTTER PLATE

Looks like this: *Is used this way:*

 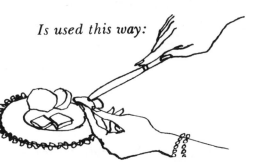

Break off bite size pieces from bread or rolls and use the small knife to butter them *as you eat them.* Do not butter a whole roll or all the pieces at one time. Breaking and buttering is done on the side of the butter plate, not over your dinner plate or under your chin where you can inspect the job. Leave the little knife on the butter plate when you are not using it.

A MAIN COURSE OF MEAT

Looks like this: *Is eaten this way:*

With the dinner fork in your left hand—its prongs down—spear and hold the meat. Cut one small piece with the dinner knife held in your right hand. Then the expert way is to lift the morsel to your mouth without changing hands or shifting the position of the fork. This is easier than shifting the fork from hand to hand as you put a forkful of meat into your mouth. However, the latter method—called the zig-zag method—is permissible until you can train your left hand to do its share of the work.

When you want to rest—or butter bread or take a drink—place your knife and fork in the rest position. When you pass your plate for more, line up the knife and fork at the right side of your plate. Both knife and fork should be on the plate together *only* when you are resting or passing your plate. At other times, either the knife or the fork should always be in hand, but should not be used like a conductor's baton while you're talking.

A FISH COURSE (OR MAIN COURSE WITH FISH)

Looks like this: *Is eaten this way:*

Usually the fish fork and the knife are both used. The knife is held in quite a different way from a regular knife. The fork is held in the left hand and the prongs should always be down. The knife cuts and pushes the fish onto the back of the fork which is then lifted, as is, to the mouth. If the fish is soft and boneless, use the fork only and keep it in your right hand, using prongs up. Leave the knife on the table.

A SALAD COURSE OR SALAD PLATE

Looks like this when it is served after the main course:

Looks like this when it is served along with the main course:

Use only the salad fork, but if there are large, hard-to-cut, pieces, use the salad knife, too. Always eat from the salad plate and never transfer salad to your dinner plate. When salad is served along with the main course, there may be no salad fork or knife, so you eat it with your dinner fork. When you are finished with a salad fork, place it on the salad plate with the prongs up.

A DESSERT COURSE

Is eaten this way: *this way:*   *or this way:*

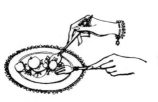

Desserts are probably your favorite foods. Most desserts are easy to eat, because they require only a spoon or a fork. For example, a spoon is used to eat soft or runny desserts like ice cream, puddings, custards or soufflés. But a fork is used to eat more solid desserts like pies, cakes and tarts when you will want to cut off bite-size pieces as you eat. Sometimes, however, you will be served desserts that are

29

a combination of both soft and solid ingredients: ice cream and cake, strawberry shortcake, jelly roll, éclairs, or berries with whipped cream. Because they are more complicated, they require both a fork and the spoon. These are easy to use correctly when you remember to pick up the spoon with your right hand, the fork with your left. Then you use the fork to hold the dessert in place while you cut off a bite-size piece and scoop it up with the spoon. The prongs of the fork are pointed down toward the plate and the front of the fork is turned toward you — making a little wall for the spoon to push against so your dessert won't slide off the side of the plate.

When you are served fresh fruit for dessert, you may eat it with your fingers when it is something small like cherries, grapes, plums or apricots. But if the fruit is large and juicy like peaches, pears, or apples, it is better to cut it into pieces before you pick it up with your fingers. If there is danger of juice dripping, use a knife and fork instead of fingers.

A FINGERBOWL IS SOMETIMES SERVED

Sometimes fingerbowls are presented, because fruit and other stains can never be removed from napkins. So before you wipe your fingers, dip them into the fingerbowl and then blot them on the napkin.

If there is a dessert knife, fork or spoon on the plate with the fingerbowl, that means dessert or fruit will follow. So you simply rearrange the fingerbowl, along with a doily that may be under it, placing them both to the left of your plate—then put the dessert silver where it belongs: the fork to the left of your plate, the spoon to the right.

COMPLICATED FOODS

Artichokes are eaten with the fingers. Pull off the leaves one at a time, dip them into the sauce, then pull them through your front teeth to scrape off the delicious soft part. The leaves are then put in a neat circle on your plate. When you come to the thistly part of the heart, scrape it away with your knife; cut and eat the heart with a fork dipping each piece into the sauce.

Asparagus (fresh) can be eaten with your fingers but it is often messy. It is better to use your fork to cut off the tender parts and then dip them into the sauce. You may bite off any edible parts remaining on the ends by holding them in your fingers, not on your fork.

Baked potatoes are buttered and blended, bite by bite, with your fork, the prongs up while you're doing it. Same for the skin, although you use your knife to cut it after it's buttered.

Berries are eaten with a spoon. But when strawberries are served with their stems, hold the stem while you dip the strawberry in the sugar. The stem never leaves your fingers until it is placed on the side of your plate.

31

Candy in frilled papers is picked up frill and all, from a plate or a box. Always take the piece nearest you and the one you touch first. Put the frill aside, naturally.

Corn on the cob is buttered, salted and eaten a few rows at a time. If you butter an entire ear all at once, it drips all over. Use both hands with corn.

Lobster and hard-shelled crabs are cracked with a nutcraker, usually before being served. Use a seafood fork, or nut pick, to extract the meat from the shell and from the claws. If the claw meat comes out in one large piece, cut it with your fork. All pieces are dipped in sauce with the fork. The "Coral" roe and green "Tamale" in the lobster's middle are delicious, so don't skip them.

Sticky cake is eaten with a fork. Dry cake, pound cake and fruit cake are broken off in small pieces and eaten with your fingers.

Spaghetti is quieter and less messy if you wind it around a dinner fork held against a large spoon. The Italian peasants do it this way.

While reading this chapter, you probably said to yourself, "How can I possibly remember all of these rules?" The simple answer is that you can't—unless you use good table manners all of the time and not reserve them for special occasions. It would be helpful for you to re-read this chapter every once in a while to refresh your memory.

Naturally you won't be eating very complicated foods all of the time and will forget a few of the special rules. When that happens to you—stop, take a sip of water and glance around to see what other people are doing. Watching and listening can be your best teacher.

Chapter III

PARTIES

Going to Them and Giving Them

Most of the parties you attend now are birthday parties. When you are older, you will go to, and give, dinner parties, receptions, teas and dances.

The rules of politeness and manners for birthday parties now are just the same as they will be for grown up parties later. Therefore, it is important to learn exactly what to do and how to act at any party. Once you learn how to be a good guest, you will find that you have more fun at parties; and that you'll be invited more often because people enjoy having you more.

ACCEPTING THE INVITATION

Sometimes you will receive an invitation by card in the mail; other times you will be invited by telephone. If the invitation is written, it will usually have your hostess' telephone number on it so that you can easily call her and tell her whether or not you can attend. You should always answer an invitation as soon as you can, because your hostess will want to know if you are coming. If you can't

34

go to a party, maybe she would like to invite someone to take your place.

Before you accept an invitation ask your mother's permission. She will want to know as soon as possible to help you select a birthday gift and anything you might need like new gloves or party shoes. She must arrange to get you to and from the party. Almost every time she will agree that you can go. But if she says "No," and you are disappointed, it is poor manners to make a fuss about it. Perhaps she has planned a lesson or a doctor's appointment for you. After all, there will be other parties, and sometimes you have to fit your plans to the family's.

If you can go, call the friend who invited you right away. Never say you'll let her know later! Surely you have heard your mother accept invitations by telephone, so it shouldn't be too difficult to be just as ladylike as she is.

Pretend your name is Jackie, and your friend's is Mary. Dial the number, keeping your mind on what you are doing. When someone answers, speak clearly and say, "Hello, this is Jackie calling. May I speak to Mary, please?" If Mary is in, you can tell her the good news at once. If she is not in, say that you will call again later, and remember to say "goodbye" before hanging up.

If you hear about a party to which you are not invited, you must not ask for an invitation. Perhaps your friend can have only a limited number of guests this time, and you'll be on her list for the next party.

SENDING INVITATIONS

First make a guest list, keeping in mind the number of people you and your family can entertain comfortably. Your favorite friends will naturally be first on the list; remember the gayest parties are usually those where people know each other. Include some newcomers; they can become your very good friends—but you will have to pay a little more attention to them until they feel at home with your old friends.

Invitations should go out a week before the party, at your age. (Later, when you are grown-up, it will be necessary to extend invitations farther ahead than one week if it is a busy time of year, like the Christmas season.) Written invitations leave less chance for mistakes in address, time and place. However, you may telephone if you are ready to give all the facts carefully and slowly. Always mention the kind of party being planned—birthday, bowling, swimming, movie, picnic—so that guests will know what to wear and what to expect.

THE PARTY

Answering the Door. The hostess opens the door wide, stands aside and lets the guest enter, saying, "Hello, Jackie, please come in," or just, "Come in." If you are the guest at a birthday party, say "Happy Birthday!" as you enter.

Introductions. If you are the hostess, your mother or some other adult should be near the door with you until all guests have been greeted. Introduce each guest to your mother and any grown-ups standing with you. When you are the guest, speak first to the grown-up, "Hello, Mrs. Smith," and then to your friend.

After introductions, a guest who is wearing a coat should be told where to leave it.

Gifts. Give your friend the birthday gift you've brought as you enter the house. It should have a card with your

name on it so your hostess can remember each gift and thank her friends properly.

When it is your birthday party, you must say "Thank you," as you are handed each gift at the door. You may either open the package immediately or put it aside to be opened along with the others when everyone has arrived. A second "thank you" must be said when you open the gift. Even if it is not your first choice, you must not show disappointment. Good manners mean kindness, and being unhappy about a gift would surely hurt your friend's feelings.

Meeting other guests. When you are the hostess, be certain everyone at the party meets everyone else. "Jackie, this is Bobby Williams—Jackie Jones." When you see the guest, you simply say "How do you do," as you are introduced. You may also just say "hello," the main rule is say *something*.

Party games. Party games should be fun. Try to be enthusiastic about the games planned. Be a good sport. Don't be upset if you're not chosen to play first or if you don't win. Remember the hostess plans the games and the rules, so save any personal suggestions and opinions for the party you have at your house.

When you are the hostess and win a game, don't keep the prize but automatically—and gracefully—give it to the second-place player.

Keeping the party going. When you are a guest among new people, don't stand in the corner or whisper to the one person you know well. When you are the hostess, talk to each of your guests frequently during the party. You must see that no one is left out of the fun or games.

Refreshments. The food and drinks are usually the part

38

people enjoy most at parties. Decoration, food (certainly the birthday cake!), flowers and color schemes make the party table special. As gay as the crowd is, you must remember your table manners even when wearing a crazy party hat, or opening the amusing favor at your place. Never push your way into the dining room. It's best to wait for everyone to be seated and for your hostess to start eating before you do.

When you are the hostess, pass the food to your guests before serving yourself. Don't make remarks about your guests' eating habits or table manners.

As a guest, don't overload your plate. When you are offered a second helping, you say "No, thank you" or "Yes, please." Handle food carefully to keep it off furniture, rugs and your own clothes. When you are not seated at a table for refreshments, carry your plate of food very carefully. If an accident occurs and you spill or drop something, try to do what you can to clean it up but don't make a big fuss about it and embarrass everyone. Neither do you act as if it were the biggest joke or stunt in the whole world.

When you wish to leave the table for any reason, you don't have to give an explanation. Simply say "Excuse me" and leave. Do not take your napkin with you, but place it on your chair until you return.

SAYING GOODBYE

Usually the time the party is to be over is written on the invitation. If not, you will notice the others starting to leave—a good sign that it's time for you to say goodbye too. If you are supposed to call your mother to be picked up, ask your hostess' mother for permission to use the telephone.

As you leave, always say "Goodbye" and "Thank you" to both your hostess and her mother. You must say, "Goodbye, Mrs. Brown, and thank you." Then, "Thanks, Mary, and goodbye," or "Goodbye, Mary, it was nice of you to invite me" or simply "Goodbye, Mary, it was fun."

You should never linger after the other guests have gone. A party is planned usually for two or three hours. At the end of the party, guests are supposed to leave so the host or hostess can clean up.

When you are the hostess, your goodbye to each guest is as important as your hello. You must be on hand at the door as each guest is ready to leave. Don't wander away and leave the goodbyes to your mother. Your attention belongs to your guests right up to the time they are on their way home.

You shouldn't thank a guest for coming to the party but you do say "Goodbye," adding "It was fun," or "So glad you came" or "Thanks again for the present." What you say should be brief and express what you naturally feel.

Chapter IV

GOING PLACES
AND DOING THINGS

Special treats are the most exciting! You are taken to a big, public place like a theater, museum, restaurant or concert hall. Often it's crowded with people; sometimes it will be entirely new to you. It is easy to forget that others are there for the same reason you are: to have fun, to be entertained or to relax.

Young ladies must learn how to be proper hostesses, but when you go to public places it is the gentleman who takes over. Boys of your age probably won't be attending the theater or visiting a restaurant without an adult. However, in a few more years you will be going to these places, and often taking a young lady with you. Watching your father's behavior can teach you a great deal. You can practice on your sister! Frequently, you will be taken out to lunch, dinner or to the theater by your mother, aunt or grandmother. They would be delighted if you pulled out their chairs and help them take off their coats.

There are some simple Do's and Dont's that will guarantee you a good time and an invitation to go again:

AT THE MOVIES

If you arrive after the lights are out, wait a second at the back of the theater until your eyes are adjusted to the darkness. Then you can find a seat without stepping on people's feet.

To find seats, a boy always goes down the aisle in front of the girl to look for seats. He then steps aside and lets the girl or woman enter the row of seats first. If there is an usher, it is just the reverse: The boy follows behind the girl.

When you have to pass in front of others to get to your seats, say "Please excuse me," or "I beg your pardon" or "I'm sorry,"—never just "Pardon" or "Pardon me." Say it to the first person in the row and all the others you pass until you reach your seat. While doing this, face the screen or stage not the people you're disturbing.

When others pass in front of you, make yourself as small as possible. Better still, stand up and let others go by without too much squeezing. You say "Certainly" when the person says "Please excuse me."

When you have something to say, whisper, but do so as little as possible. If you have seen the movie before, don't spoil it for others by telling them what is to happen. If you aren't enjoying a section of the movie, try not to ruin it for *others* who might think it's just great.

Popcorn and candy bars are as much a part of movies as the film, but they should be eaten neatly and privately.

Loud laughter, humming, whistling, gum snapping or big

talk belong on the playground, not in a quiet place where everyone has paid admission to listen.

THEATER, BALLET, CONCERTS

In all three, the artists are ALIVE on the stage performing for you. It is terribly impolite to arrive late for a performance. Try to get there a little early, not just in the nick of time. It's an insult to arrive late; just the same as if they were your hosts at dinner and you arrived after everyone had started eating.

Ushers usually lead you to your seats after your father (or an adult) hands them all of the tickets. When the usher leads you to your seats, the ladies follow immediately behind the usher and after them, the gentlemen. If there is no usher, your father takes the place of the usher as you walk down the aisle, and waits for the women and girls to enter the row of seats first.

If the performance has already started, the usher decides whether to wait until there is a pause in the program to seat you. Ladies always go in first, gentlemen second. The gentleman should help the ladies remove their coats, trying not to disturb people around them. The programs are usually handed to the adult who distributes them when you are all seated.

Intermission is the time you may leave your seat. It is usually a 10 to 15 minute period during which you can get a drink of water, go to the rest room or visit with friends.

Applause is your way of thanking the artists for their performance. You applaud at the end of each act in a play. But at a concert or a ballet you only applaud at special times: when the conductor walks on stage and bows to the audience, and when each musical or dance selection is completed. Most music has several different parts with pauses in between—like chapters in a book—so it is wiser to watch the conductor. He will turn to face the audience when the selection is finished.

Boys and girls applaud differently. A boy claps with the palms of his hands flat; but a girl forms a shallow cup of her left hand and "spanks" it with her right hand.

Until the performance is entirely over, do not begin putting on your things. If you have to leave the theater during one of the acts to go to the rest rooms, or if you begin to cough, say "Please excuse me" when you pass in front of those who are seated and leave as quietly as possible. When you return to your seat be as unnoticeable as possible.

EATING OUT

When you go to a restaurant, everything looks, tastes and seems better than at home. Even your table manners will be easier to remember and manage. But there are a few different things to know about restaurant behavior:

You wait to be seated. Except at a counter, you wait at the entrance for a Hostess or Headwaiter to assign your family to a table. The ladies of the family always follow the headwaiter, with the men following behind. If there is no Hostess or Headwaiter, the father or adult goes first to find a suitable table.

Women and girls are seated first. Their chairs are pulled out by either the waiter or by the father for the mother and by the boy for his sister. Your father will help your mother and sister off with their coats but if you are with your mother or aunt, pull out her chair and help her off

with her coat. A man never takes his hat and coat to the table; they are always checked before entering the dining room.

You receive a menu from the waiter and study it while waiting for your parents' suggestions. A man does the ordering for everyone in his family after asking what each person prefers.

Only your father may call the waiter's attention. He may

lift his hand until the waiter's eye is attracted or if the waiter is close to your table, he may say "Waiter," "Head-waiter," or "Captain," or "Miss" to the hostess. When you are out to dinner with adults, let them speak to the waiter for you.

You all probably visit your local ice-cream parlor or sweet shop and when ordering never call the waiter's attention with "Hey," or "Boy" or "Psst."

You do not thank waiters for each dish they bring you. But if a waiter asks you a question concerning the food, answer "Yes, please" or "No, thank you." A tip is left by your father at the end of the meal as a thank you for the service.

You do not pick up anything you drop from the table. Leave it on the floor. The waiter will pick up any dropped implements after you leave. Ask for another knife or fork if you need one.

When someone comes to the table to talk a boy always rises to his feet and remains standing while the other person is present. A girl remains seated, except when an older woman stops to talk.

Gloves, purses and handkerchiefs stay off the table. Place them on your lap or under your chair throughout the meal.

Glasses are not fingerbowls—so fingers or napkins should never be dipped in them.

Your napkin and chair. Leave the napkin crumpled, not re-folded, at the left of your plate. It is thoughtful to push your chair slightly under the table instead of leaving it in the passage way. You don't have to excuse yourself when you are finished, the way you do at home. Wait until everyone else has finished before getting up. Never leave with food in your mouth. A restaurant is a busy place and

47

it is a help to leave without causing extra work for anyone. The men precede the ladies out of the dining room or restaurant. At the outside door, the man holds the door for the ladies until they have stepped outside.

Have fun—but don't shout across the room, run around the tables or talk as if you were alone in the restaurant.

IN CHURCH

The reason you attend church is to become a better person. Your religion helps you to know the difference between right and wrong and guides you toward being kinder and more understanding to your family and friends.

Many of your friends probably attend different churches from yours and have different religions. All churches—whether Protestant, Catholic or Jewish—are quiet, calm and orderly. You show respect to your church or to your friend's church by having good manners when attending a service.

Be on time. Be a few minutes early if possible, so that you can select the seats you prefer. If you happen to be late, wait a few minutes at the back of the church until the usher directs you to a seat.

Wear simple, serious clothes — not play clothes or "fad" clothes. Be neat, clean and uncluttered. Boys should always wear ties, girls should wear hats. A boy removes his hat in the vestibule of the church.

When you go down the aisle of a church, the father always goes first, followed by his family. He stands aside while the family enters the pew and takes the aisle seat. In the absence of his father, the oldest son goes first and takes his father's place. Otherwise, a boy's mother and sisters go down the aisle ahead of him and enter the pew first.

48

Stop talking even before you enter the church. Save any conversation, comments or questions until after you have left the church.

Sit quietly — without books, games or gadgets to fill the time. When you giggle, fidget or whisper in church, you disturb people on all sides of you. Even if you don't fully understand, listen and watch and try to follow along by reading the service.

In a strange church, don't criticize or question what is happening *WHILE* it is happening. If you are confused about sitting, standing or kneeling, wait and do as others do. Find out about the customs and rituals later.

Attentiveness in Sunday School will help you to eventually become a full member of your church—someone who understands the meaning and purpose of the service. Remember that most Sunday School teachers give their time in order to teach you about the Bible and its remarkable history. Listen to them—they are a wonderful way to learn about your religion.

VISITING

One of the nicest compliments is to be asked to visit a friend's house for an overnight visit or a weekend! There is no better way to get acquainted or to have fun.

When you accept the invitation you do so only when you are sure the invitation came from the mother of your friend, too! (Just ask, "Is it all right with your mother?") Be sure to check with your mother, too. Even if it is a neighbor inviting you to stay overnight, find out exactly when you are supposed to arrive and depart. There will be no misunderstandings or difficulties about transportation that way.

Pack your suitcase. Remember to include everything you will need from morning to night—from your toothbrush to your bedtime slippers. Be sure you check your suitcase before you leave. Try not to borrow personal items unless you definitely find it necessary to. It is a nice gesture to select a small gift for your friend's mother if your visit will be longer than one day and night.

When you arrive at the house unpack your suitcase and organize your things so you will be able to find them all again at the end of the visit. Be willing and eager to follow the customs of the home you are visiting. Perhaps mealtimes, bedtime or bath times are different from yours. In that case, go along with the routine without criticizing or comparing it with your own family's. After all, the fun of visiting is to enjoy something new!

When you are served new foods or foods you don't like, take a little and taste it. It isn't proper to say, "We never eat that" or "We always go to bed later." In a friend's home, obey his or her family's rules, no matter how different they are from your own rules at home.

While you are visiting in someone else's home don't investigate it. Private possessions, letters, closed doors or closets are out-of-bounds for you. Wouldn't it be embarrassing to be discovered looking in someone elses drawer? Give the same thoughtfulness to others' furniture, floors, walls and toys that you would give your own. Help take care of the house: keep your belongings in place, offer to make your own bed in the morning even if there is a maid and make sure the bathroom you use is neat as a pin when you leave it—and don't take too much time in it.

Join in the fun. Take part in the games and entertainment planned by your hostess. You'll learn some new ones to talk about at home! If you get homesick, read a book, write a letter or suggest one of your favorite games. No one likes a house guest who keeps asking, "*NOW* what will we do?" as if the hours were dragging.

When you're hungry, don't raid the ice box, cookie jar or coke cupboard without asking permission.

Keep family secrets. It's fun to get acquainted with a new family, but you don't have to tell everything—good or bad —about your own! Gossip and unpleasant stories don't get you invited back.

Ask to use the telephone. Even for local calls, ask your friend's mother each time before you telephone.

If something breaks or doesn't work, don't try to hide it. Tell your friend's mother what happened, say you are sorry and remember that accidents happen in everyone's house.

When you get ready to leave, check to see that your room is neat and clean; and that all your possessions have been packed back into your suitcase. It's a nuisance to mail whatever you forget.

Leave when you said you were going to. Even if you're having a wonderful time, don't ask to call your mother for permission to stay on, even if your friend is urging you to stay.

When you say goodbye, say it to your friend's parents and to every member of the family. Don't forget a maid or cook who did extra work while you were there; take a minute to say goodbye and thank her.

When you get home, write a thank-you note to your friend's mother within a few days, saying what a fine time you had. It is always nice to also write a note to your friend.

Chapter V

GOOD GROOMING CAN BE FUN

The little beauty we're talking about is *you* — especially when you're well-groomed, healthy and happy. Although you are beginning to look just the way you will as a teen-ager and later, as an adult, you will continue to change—every season and year—only to become lovelier and more graceful if you want to! It's really easy, if you follow these basic, every-day steps toward beauty and better grooming.

YOUR HAIR

People call hair "your crowning glory" because your hair makes everything about your face look prettier. Your hair has roots just as trees do, and like trees or plants, hair needs food, water and fresh air to keep growing. When you brush and shampoo your hair, you keep it shiny and soft. Above all, eating the correct foods—eggs, butter, cheese, fruit, meat, green vegetables—keeps your hair healthy and you full of energy.

Brush daily. Every night before you go to sleep, brush your hair 100 strokes, using a natural bristle brush because it takes out snarls without snapping off the ends of your hair. To make brushing more relaxing, lie across your bed, face down; then slowly brush down from the top of your head to the ends of your hair. Switch the brush from one hand to another after 50 strokes—in that way your arms will not get tired. When you're finished, put your hair brush in a drawer to keep it away from dust.

Shampoo once a week. Before you start to wash your hair, give it a thorough brushing to remove tangles. To prevent getting soap in your eyes, you can wear terry cloth goggles or a shampoo shield with a brim around your face—in that way you can see what you are doing. A shower is perhaps easiest, but a bathtub or wash basin will do just as well, especially if you connect a special spray-hose to the faucet.

First, wet your hair, then put a little shampoo in one hand and rub it into your scalp. Massage the scalp well, rinse with warm water, and shampoo again, working up a thick lather. Then, rinse thoroughly. Now try the "Squeak Test": Pull a strand of hair through your fingers. If it squeaks, it's clean. If not, repeat the shampoo and rinse once more. If you are using the wash basin, fill a plastic glass with water to rinse your hair and make sure all the soap is out. Remember, use very little shampoo because too much soap makes hair dull and dry.

When you are sure your hair is clean and rinsed, take a small brush and scrub around your hairline to remove soap or dirt you might have missed. This will keep pimples and rashes away.

Dry-shampoo if necessary. This is a trick for the times you have a cold and can't wash your hair. Slip your hairbrush into one of your mother's old nylon stockings and brush the dirt from your hair onto the stocking. Another dry-shampoo trick: Stick dabs of absorbent cotton in the bristles of your hairbrush. They will not only remove the stickiness and dirt, but will make your hair shiny and soft.

Make a towel-turban. When your hair is rinsed, make a turban out of the bath towel like this: Hang your head forward and pull the towel tightly around your head. Now twist the ends into a rope to tighten the towel around your forehead. Then toss your head back quickly and flip the ends of the towel over your head.

Wash your comb and brush every time you wash your hair. First, remove the matted hair from the brush, by combing it out of the bristles. Then swish the comb and brush in soapy water with ammonia in it, rinse them, and put them aside to dry while you rub your hair dry.

Brush your hair before it's completely dry. Make a part with the comb, and brush out all the tangles. If you want to train your hair to turn under, brush the tip ends over the palm of your hand. If you want a pretty dip on the side, place your hand over that section of hair, spread your fingers apart and then press them together to make the hair loop in the middle. If you want your bangs to go a certain way, comb them while they're still damp, then put a pretty hair net or sleep-cap over your head and forehead to keep the bangs in place while they dry.

Turn the page to see five hair styles you can wear.

BANGS—especially good for short or curly hair and for girls with high foreheads.

PONY TAIL—Never use a rubber band on a pony tail. It splits ends and thins your hair. Use a thin strip of leather or a barrette. Always remove clips at bedtime.

BARRETTE OR RIBBON BOW—*The barrette for school wear; the ribbon bow for parties.*

LONG STYLE—*With a head band for medium or long hair. Hair brushed off the forehead guarantees a pretty, even hair line when you're older.*

BRAIDS—*Someone will have to make the braids for you, but you can tie your own ribbons on the ends. They are so comfortable and cool in the summer and leave lovely waves in your hair. Never sleep with braids—it's a tug-of-war between your hair and head.*

57

YOUR DAILY BATH

Bathing should make your skin soft as well as clean. Bubble baths are the most fun. Baths should be leisurely, but not at the price of excluding other members of your family from the bathroom if there is only one. To be considerate of others, take showers to save time when others are waiting.

When you get in the tub, start washing at the top: Wash your face with soap, counting to 60 while you move the washcloth in circles from neck to forehead. Wash your ears carefully. To keep soap out of your hair, pull it up into a quick pony tail or wear a shower cap. Then really

rinse off all the soap. Otherwise, your skin will be dry and chapped.

Always use a nail brush as part of your bath—it's the only way to clean fingernails, toenails, elbows and heels.

To keep your nails from cracking and breaking, eat fish, eggs and Jello, and have plenty of sun.

After you're all dry (even between your toes) use bath powder with a big puff so you can reach around to your back. The only perfume you should use is bath talcum, so puff it on generously.

YOUR TEETH

Someday you will wear lipstick. Then strong, white teeth will be especially important. So brush properly at least twice a day and your smile will be glowing. An electric toothbrush not only does a better job, but it does all the work for you. Whatever kind of brush you have, use it the way dentists suggest. Start by brushing your back teeth. Then brush the sides and front—inside, too!—with up-and-down motions, never sideways, across the teeth. Rinse your mouth with water, or with mouthwash mixed with water and gargle.

Once a week, whiten your teeth by brushing them with a mixture of one teaspoon of soda and one teaspoon of salt. The taste isn't very good, but the shiny whiteness is! Drinking milk, eating crunchy vegetables, bread and cereals will keep your teeth healthy and prevent cavities. Also, try to limit the amount of sweets you eat.

YOUR FINGERNAILS

You're old enough now to have a manicure kit, or to make one of your own out of any little box. You will need a nail clipper, an emery board—which is a soft sandpaper file—some cotton or tissue and, of course, a nail brush.

The first step is to trim the nails carefully with a nail clippers. Clippers have just the right amount of curve, they're less dangerous than scissors, and they can be used in either hand.

Next, file off any rough edges with an emery board. For a manicure, soak your fingers in a bowl of warm, soapy water to soften the cuticle at the base of each fingernail. Then dry your hands and gently push the cuticle back down where it belongs. This makes your nails neater and longer-looking. Draw a little while pencil under the tip of each nail to make it look clean and white.

When you're older the last step will be nail polish, but until you're twelve or thirteen years old, keep polish off your nails, and when you do wear it later, keep it light.

HOW TO BE WELL DRESSED

Good manners teach you how to act politely. And good grooming habits teach you how to be clean, healthy and bright. Now you are ready to learn how to dress well, because there is a big difference between being well dressed and just having clothes on. For example, you had all the right clothes on, the morning you first shouted, "Look, I got dressed all by myself!" But one part was on backward, another inside-out, and your shoes were on the wrong feet!

At that moment, you learned that clothes can look right or wrong. And that you can be comfortable and happy in some, but uncomfortable and unsure in others. You are already beginning to have favorite clothes and colors. And as you grow up, you will gradually develop your own style in clothes. You will know exactly what you like to wear most and what you look best in. For the time being, however, you are too young to go out and buy your own clothes. And you're not ready to take complete care of them—to wash, iron or sew properly. But you *can* learn

how to help choose and care for your clothes in a more grown-up way. These are things you can do, to be well-dressed, regardless of how many clothes you have or where you will wear them:

You can help select your clothes. Whenever possible, after the age of six or seven, you can take an interest in the many styles, colors and fabrics when you and your parents go shopping for your clothes. Try on what seems best; then listen to the advice of your mother or the sales person. You will soon learn what you should wear and why. Your first choices may not always be right, but with practice you'll realize that good taste means:

Clothes that are comfortable to wear, and ones that don't need constant fussing or tugging at.
Clothes that are simple in line, color and trim.
Clothes that fit well, are easy to get into and out of.
Clothes that are the right length—two inches above the knees for girls until they are twelve years old. Shorter, they look babyish; longer, they look sad.

You can help care for your clothes and room because when your room is in order, and your clothes are in good condition, you can be well-dressed in half the time. Learn to:

Hang up clean clothes that can be worn again.

Place soiled clothes in the laundry basket.

Use skirt hangers to avoid ugly creases and wrinkles in skirts and slacks.

Keep your dresser drawers in order, with socks rolled and in pairs, and with a place for each kind of clothing: underwear, sweaters, blouses, accessories.

Arrange your closet sensibly. Hang separates first, then dresses, then jackets or coats. At a glance you will be able to decide and prepare your outfit for the next day or occasion.

Keep clothes off the floor. Pick up things as you step out of them. You'll have more time for fun and sports if you spend a minute or two every day to put away and hang up clothes. But you'll have a messy job ahead if you let discarded clothes accumulate around the room.

Polish or clean your shoes at least twice a week. With the new shoe polishes, it is a matter of a few seconds— and it's fun to do. Remember that other people notice your shoes more than you do, because moving feet attract attention. And dirty or dull shoes can spoil the whole effect of a perfect outfit.

You can learn what to wear. Even though there are new fads every year, these are the basic guides to being well-dressed:

For School — Wear conservative, simple jumpers or separate skirts with blouses or sweaters in matching or contrasting colors. Try to keep to two or three colors only when you select your school clothes. In that way, all parts are interchangeable. Dark green, blue, red or brown are the preferable basic colors.

For the last two months of school in the spring, choose cotton dresses and separates that will go on into the summer for play wear and shopping.

Have at least one button-down cardigan to coordinate with your skirts and dresses.

Select one all-weather coat or jacket. It can be a raincoat, but it should have a hood or a matching hat.

Alternate your clothes even though you may have favorites. Don't wear the same dress or outfit too many days in a row. You'll get more wear and pleasure from your clothes if you give them a rest between school days.

For Play — Choose sturdy, easy to wash clothes that you won't be afraid will tear or get dirty.

Slacks, jeans and shorts in bright or dark colors are perfect, but not if they're skin-tight and only if they're worn for play, sports and the beach. They should not be worn shopping or in town, no matter how good they are.

Remember to change your shoes as well as your school clothes when you play. And reserve sneakers for play wear, not for the classroom.

For Parties — You need at least two good party dresses, which should be kept for party and Sunday wear. In summer high waisted organdy or organza, eyelet cotton or any of the starchy pastel cottons are fine. In winter, lace-collared velveteen or velvet is elegant. Shiny, satiny fabrics should be avoided even for party wear.

Your dress-up coat should fit loosely enough to go over full-skirted party dresses without wrinkling them.

Your petticoats should be bought one size smaller than your dress size; so they won't hang below your dress.

63

A white cardigan is almost a necessity to wear over party dresses when it's too warm for a coat.

Party shoes should be black patent leather in the fall and winter; white in the spring and summer, with flat heels and little straps.

No party dress is complete without a hat, white gloves and a purse to match or blend with your party shoes. And in the purse: handkerchief, comb, and a change purse.

Jewelry should be limited to a charm bracelet, a birthstone ring, perhaps a fine gold chain necklace with a pearl, locket or cross. But no gaudy or jangly jewelry until you're a teen-ager.

CONCLUSION

Now you've reached the end of this book, but really it's the beginning for you. And anytime you have any questions, come back to the book. Keep it handy so it will always be there to help you with your white gloves and party manners.